D0165884

You too can grow Bonsai

BONSAI
with Australian Native Plants

Dorothy & Vita Koreshoff

Illustrations by
Dorothy & Vita Koreshoff

Photography by Penny Turner

The Bonsai that have been photographed for this book are only a small part of our Native collection, and although all the species that we have listed in the book exist as Bonsai in our collection, it is not possible to reproduce photographs of them all in a book of this size.

We have tried to choose varieties that will be of interest to the reader.

Bonsai are not an easy subject for the Photographer and we would like to acknowledge the talent of Penny Turner.

 Published by Boolarong Publications

Other Books by the Authors:
Bonzai in Australia
Bonzai in the Tropics
Bonsai in New Zealand

First published in 1983 by Boolarong Publications
12 Brookes Street, Bowen Hills, Brisbane, Qld 4006.
Reprinted in 1984.
Reprinted in 1985.
Reprinted in 1986.
Reprinted in 1987.
Reprinted in December, 1987.
Reprinted in April, 1989.
Reprinted in June, 1990.
Reprinted April, 1991.
Reprinted April, 1992.

Copyright © Dorothy & Vita Koreshoff.

This book is copyright. Apart from any fair dealing for
the purposes of private study, research, criticism or
review, as permitted under the Copyright Act, no part
may be reproduced by any process without written
permission. Inquiries should be addressed to the
Publishers.

All rights reserved.

National Library of Australia
Cataloguing-in-Publication data.

   Koreshoff, Dorothy.
     You too can grow bonsai: bonsai with
     Australian native plants.

   ISBN 0 908175 66 3.

   1. Bonsai — Australia. I. Koreshoff, Vita.
   II. Title.

6359'772

BOOLARONG PUBLICATIONS
12 Brookes Street, Bowen Hills, Brisbane, Qld 4006.

Design, reproduction and phototypesetting by
Press Etching (Qld.) Pty Ltd, Brisbane.
Printed and bound by Watson Ferguson, Brisbane.

COVER PHOTO
Rulingia hermanifolia.
Originated from tubed nursery stock in 1975 and potted into a training pot for
at least two years. It was intended for an informal upright, but the lower
branches grew so vigorously that it was decided to take advantage of this
characteristic and develop it into a Cascade.

Contents

List of Suitable Varieties

Varieties in Brief

Introduction

Until recently, trees indigenous to Australia have either been ignored or feared by Bonsai growers. Lately interest seems to be increasing, but due, in many instances to lack of information on the subject, the grower is unsuccessful, and does not pursue this interesting facet of Bonsai.

Our experience with Natives goes back to 1949. We had removed a very thick buttressed plant with promising Bonsai shape from a crevice between rocks and had it identified as Ficus rubiginosa, the Port Jackson Fig. This started us off, initially with an interest in Figs, which developed into a greater enthusiasm for the possibilities of finding aged trees, waiting to become 'instant Bonsai'.

In Japan, the famous pedigreed Bonsai were the result of collecting very old specimens from the wild, so the incentive really, to grow Australian Plants was more for that reason, than the love of the species.

Well, — the best laid plans etc. — There were suitably impressive old plants to be found, but all our attempts other than Figs, proved to be unsuccessful until 1956.

In that year we saw she-oaks, Casuarina cunninghamiana, growing along the edges of the Nepean River (60 km west of Sydney). These trees had been constantly cropped by grazing cattle. With little effort we were able to lift them with masses of feeder roots close to the trunk. At the same time we observed Coast Myall Wattles, Acacia glaucescens, growing on sand bars in the same stream. We successfully removed three for trial, and returned some months later to obtain more, only to find the sand bar and the trees on it had been swept away during recent floods.

Advocating the removal of specimens from the wild could cause arguments with conservationists, and we agree that indiscriminate, mass digging of plants, doomed to die for lack of care or knowledge is wrong. Also, one should be aware that some areas are restricted for the removal of plants, and other places are possible with permission.

More argument could arise with the question, 'What is an Australian Native?' Of course the purists will insist that it definitely cannot include the cultivars, however, we have included some in the list of varieties as we feel that this is the information the majority of readers are seeking.

chapter 1

Are Natives hardy?

There are many Native varieties that are as hardy and able to withstand the root pruning exercise as easily as some exotics. This may surprise many, for the popular belief over the years has been that natives are touchy, and cannot be easily removed, transplanted or rootpruned.

Without help and advice, one may experience many failures and lose time. Hopefully, this book will help you understand some of their requirements.

As there is a very great interest in growing Australian Plants, indeed, the Society For Growing Australian Plants has one of the largest memberships in this country, their aim often being the collecting and growing as many species, or varieties of particular species as possible. After a time, the variety is planted from the tube into a larger container where it continues to grow healthily for a few more years or until the pot has become rootbound. Unless the plant continues to be 'potted on', it gradually begins to deteriorate. This also helps to encourage the belief that Natives are temperamental. The horticultural techniques which are applied to Bonsai in order that they may attain great age, but still remain HEALTHY, can well be used by growers of any plants that are containerized. This means that by rootpruning, one may keep the plant in a certain sized pot for the rest of its life, and more importantly, keeping it HEALTHY. For growers of Australian Plants, the artistic aspects of styling etc. need not be applied, but all plants respond to some pruning, so by giving an artistic haircut, the appearance of your specimens can be greatly improved.

chapter 2

Similarity between Natives and Exotics

Not only do we wish to highlight the differences, but show the many similarities between Natives and Exotics, and maybe convince you that in some cases, there is very little difference at all.

Further on, we are explaining the techniques for growing some varieties, but we feel that once you have mastered the general principles for growing Bonsai, and can realise the importance of timing (swelling of leaf buds prior to opening) for successful root-pruning, then you will be able to forget they are Natives, and think of them as additional suitable material for Bonsai.

There are two schools of thought on whether the term Bonsai can only be applied to plants that have been trained to the guidelines for shaping devised and used by the Japanese and Chinese for many years. Others feel that one should only shape their trees to styles that they are familiar with, or could it be nationalistic pride. Certainly, Australian trees are quite distinctive in shape and outline.

Whether this shape is attractive when condensed down to the miniature size for Bonsai is up to the individual to decide. So often, the 'natural form' is used as a means of by-passing the need for studying the guidelines of shaping, the so called 'natural form' created by the unskilled instead of being beautiful, actually takes on a more grotesque appearance.

The distinguishable features of Australian trees are branches that are more vertical than horizontal, lengthy bare sections of branches with foliage mainly on the outer ends of the branchlets, trunks that become indistinguishable above the lowest branches. The outline, a soft hemisphere.

South African trees are noted for their flat tops, whilst Tropicals for their lower branch lengths, forming huge unbrellas. The most familiar form of the Northern Hemisphere trees are the tall slender pyramidal conifers.

If you regard your plant material as the 'clay' with which you will sculpt your Bonsai, irrespective of its natural form, and origin, the shape and design that pleases you, can, in most cases, be made from most indigenous Australian trees.

chapter 3

Timing

The single most important factor for success with natives would have to be the timing for the pruning of roots.

This applies equally so with exotics, but most exotic species fall into more defined times, such as late winter–early spring which is usually around August–September, and late summer–early autumn which can be anytime from mid January to May (depending on the species) in most areas of Australia.

Our horticultural thinking has been mainly influenced by European gardening history. The northern hemisphere trees from the temperate zone help to highlight the marked difference between the four seasons. There is less change between our seasons, although there are places where the climate undergoes dramatic changes in temperature, i.e. Tasmania and east coast highlands, but there are very few natives with autumn colour and fewer that are deciduous. This makes it more difficult for the non gardener and novice to understand why, in many cases, their Native Bonsai died after rootpruning at the correct time for exotic trees.

Most of our indigenous trees grow and stop many, many times throughout the year. This factor is of great benefit to the Bonsai grower.

After seeing a show or demonstration, or reading an article on Bonsai in a magazine, one becomes very enthusiastic about starting, usually it happens to be the wrong time for most exotic plants. By browsing through a nursery, irrespective of the time of year, one can usually find a native plant 'ready to go'. In other words, the leaf buds beginning to swell, but prior to their bursting open.

chapter 4

How to recognize the right time

By observing trees you will notice that after the first flush of growth has appeared, the new leaves, after a time, will lose their soft green (or spring) colour and become darker. At the same time, the texture of the leaf will harden.

This is described as having matured.

The tree then settles into a dormant period for various lengths of time. Later, leaf buds can be observed at the base of the leaf stalks, and branch terminals, becoming more prominent. These will continue to swell, some more, some less according to variety, until a soft new growth begins to appear.

Fig. 1   *Leaf buds can be observed at the base*
of leaf stalks and branch terminals.

The time to rootprune, is just prior to the bursting of the leafbuds.

If this regrowth has caught you by surprise, and one or two SMALL sprouts appear at the TOP of the tree, then, providing rootpruning is done immediately, there should be no setback. THE MOST DANGEROUS TIME for any tree is when there is soft unmatured growth on the plant.

Be patient, allow the tree to grow through the cycle described above, and be ready and waiting next time around.

When rootpruning, if there is no excess growth to remove it is possible, and sometimes desirable with evergreen trees to cut either the whole leaf off through the stalk, or halfway through the leaf itself, especially if the leaves have been damaged. This half cut section will eventually brown and fall, and when done in conjunction with rootpruning, will balance the loss of root to the amount of foliage left to be supplied with nutriments, i.e. equalizing supply and demand.

Fig. 2   *Cut halfway through stalk or leaf.*

With some plants, especially Eucalypts, there always seems to be new growth on the tree right throughout the year. In some areas this seems to be the rule rather than the exception. You are waiting for the growth to mature so the plant can be rootpruned, but before it does, it starts to re-shoot. In these cases, one can artificially induce a dormant state by gradually reducing the water, mainly by allowing longer periods between watering, even allowing the leaves to wilt. In many cases this is sufficient to stop new growth, and a period of dormancy begins.

Fig. 3   Too Early   Right   Too Late

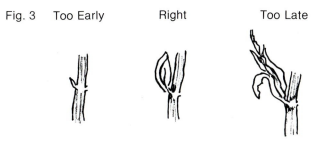

chapter 5

Obtaining plants from nurseries

More success can be guaranteed by starting with mature 2 or 3 year old nursery produced plants.

1. You are saving time as against raising seed or taking cuttings.
2. There are usually sufficient branches to provide an almost instant effect or at least to start the basic shape.
3. Most importantly, container grown trees rarely have strong tap roots, which means there should be an abundance of feeder roots present.

This makes the operation of reducing the length of the root system much more likely to be successful, and advantageous for the health and wellbeing of the tree.

Containerized plants, having been germinated and raised in a potting mixture, should not suffer any ill effects from a radical change of soil or environment.

Most wholesale nurseries carry more than half of their stock with native varieties. Many specialize in natives only. This means that there is usually an abundance of very advanced stock readily available at most retail nurseries.

chapter 6

Collecting from the wild

One important fact to bear in mind when collecting from the wild is — the older the plant, the harder it will be to change its habitat.

Some young plants can adapt quickly to a change of soil, moisture and atmosphere. Some older plants resent even the slightest change.

There can be great rewards from digging trees from the 'bush', at the same time, be prepared for many disappointments. One sees in books the massive old collected trees of Japan and America, but few realize how many trees have not survived the initial trauma of transplantation.

Keen Bonsai hunters usually keep suitable tools and equipment in their cars, but too many people upon viewing a suitable specimen, start tugging, pulling and poking with a stick, and are surprised when the tree does not 'take'.

Trees growing in moist areas give more guaranteed results. The reason should be obvious. The roots do not have to travel far in search of moisture and so, close to the trunk you find masses of feeder roots which are necessary for the survival of the transplanted tree.

The maintenance of trees from moist to wet areas poses less of a problem, than trees used to dry or arid conditions. Most Bonsai addicts tend to overwater their horticultural family anyway, and with trees requiring drier conditions, there is a fine line between killing the plant from overwatering and the dryness it should reach before rewatering.

If the variety grows in damp or wet ground, then a tray of water can be placed under the pots, especially in summer. A word of warning, if the variety grows in fresh water, make sure the water tray evaporates regularly, or tip and flush out the stale water, thus ensuring the water does not become stagnant. On the other hand, many varieties DO prefer brackish or stagnant water, so a deeper tray, kept topped up is the requirement for their wellbeing.

Plants removed from coastal environments usually fare better than plants from the interior exposed to salty conditions. Removal of plants from high, dry places such as embankments, cliffs or hilltops where subsoil water is far away, pose greater problems, and require preparation and care prior to transplanting.

Australian Natives are notorious for the vast distance the roots can travel in search of moisture, so spading around the trunk to fit a pot, eliminates any hope of success. One way to overcome the problem is to dig to spade depth, several sections around the trunk, slightly shorter than the envisaged size of pot, thus shortening at least half of the root system. Replace soil and return some months later just prior to bud opening, and spade the remaining half. If sufficient feeder roots have developed on the previous cuts, the plant could be lifted.

Fig. 4   *Dig to spade depth several sections around trunk — return. Water and spade remaining half.*

One problem exists with this method, if the area receives little rain, and is too far for periodic watering by you, then the cut roots will not regenerate, and could gradually die back. The tree though, will survive via the untrimmed roots. Nowadays there is a better method. Dan Robinson, a Bonsai enthusiast from West Coast U.S.A. thought of an idea that should work very well in our dry areas. He calls the method ROOT ENHANCEMENT which works well with old pines, which are also difficult subjects to remove from their natural environment.

Excavate the larger roots carefully to a point where there are rootlets growing. It doesn't matter how small these roots are, as long as some growth is present the method will be successful.

The rooted area is then wrapped with damp sphagnum moss which is then covered with plastic and secured at both ends. Replace the soil and allow a few months to pass before returning. When the pouch becomes filled with roots, the heavy root can be severed.

The advantages are obvious, firstly as the moisture in the pouch will be present at all times for the growing rootlets, drought conditions will not affect the tree. Also once the soil has been replaced, your work will not be ovbious. Some top pruning would be advantageous at this time.

Although, as yet, actually aerial layering the roots of pines does not seem to be working. However the possibility of its success with some Australian trees could be worth the experimentation.

Fig. 5   *Remove a ring of bark about twice the thickness of the trunk etc.*

Fig. 6   *Enlarged view of 5.*

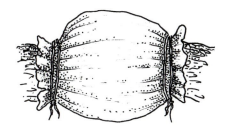

Fig. 7   *Damp sphagnum moss is wrapped around wound and covered with plastic and tied at both ends.*

chapter 7

Aerial layering

Aerial layering would be very suitable for use on branches that have characteristics suitable for Bonsai. It can also be a means of reducing the height of the trunk as well as utilizing the top section. There is also the advantage of obtaining a thicker trunk than is possible from cuttings. There has been some hesitation about the success of its use with Australian Natives. Does it work?

Fig. 8 *Used on branches that have characteristics suitable for Bonsai.*

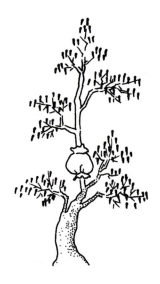

Fig. 9 *Reducing the height of trunk — top section.*

To answer this question, perhaps we should be thinking and comparing their similarities rather than their differences to exotic species. For instance, not all exotics can be layered, some are uncertain and unreliable, others take years whilst others root in only six weeks.

Starting with the Chinese, over a thousand years of practical knowledge has been obtained and compiled about its successes as well as its failures with various exotic species.

The following information may help you work out a plant's potential for layering.

GOOD RESULTS SHOULD BE OBTAINED FROM:—

.. Plants that strike well from cuttings.
2. Plants with a fine root system.
3. Plants producing aerial roots.
4. Plants that can be cut back into old wood and reshoot well.

MORE DIFFICULTY CAN BE EXPECTED FROM:—

1. Plants difficult to strike from cuttings.
2. Plants with a long, coarse root system.

These plants may respond to a different technique. Apply one or two strands of wire around the area where roots are required. Twist and tighten the wire with pliers until the wire is embedded into the bark.

Fig. 10   *One or two strands of wire around the area where roots are required.*

Wrap damp sphagnum moss around the area, and cover with polyethylene film (do not use ordinary plastic as this does not have properties to allow the gasses — oxygen and carbon dioxide to pass through) tying both ends to maintain humidity. As the tree grows and expands the tighter the wire becomes, slowly girdling the area and thus restricting the descending flow of nutriments.

At the same time the moisture travelling up the tree along an inner channel is unhindered and can continue to feed the top for as long as it takes to induce roots at the constricted point. If the plant is grown fast, quicker results can be expected.

chapter 8

Raising from seed or cuttings

In some ways, the above method can be the slowest method of all. Especially if it is grown in a small pot from the start. There are also advantages. You are controlling the plant from the beginning, creating the shape, especially in the trunk, that you desire. This slow approach produces a very refined small tree, usually without blemishes and scars from the removal of large sections.

If you wish to have medium to large Bonsai, it is advisable to grow the plant in a large container or even in the open ground until the plant reaches the trunk size that you require. Each year, at the appropriate time for the species, it should be lifted, rootpruned and top pruned and returned to the ground (pot) for another year, at the same time making sure an adequate fertilizing program is applied.

Below is a general guide for propagating your own stock:—

All the native species produce viable seed.

Cultivars are developed from cuttings.

Because of environmental conditions, Australian plants raised from seed develop long, strong tap roots, which are better removed at an early stage. This will encourage feeder roots to grow close to the trunk.

There is great variation in the methods required to induce germination of native seed. The very hard seeds need to have boiling water poured over them and allowed to soak for a few days until the moisture penetrates the coating. They should be planted while still moist. Others split open after being placed very close to a fire. Fleshy fruit/berries should be planted immediately they ripen. and be kept just slightly moist until spring. Other fruits can be soaked in water for a few days until they start to ferment, simulating the acid reaction of passing through a bird's intestines, then collected and dried and stored in a paper bag until sowing time.

In the Varieties section we include the requirements for each species.

chapter 9

Soil – potting mixture

The importance of a correct mixture for your natives to GROW and develop HEALTHILY, cannot be emphasized enough. The soil we use for exotic Bonsai is also suitable for most container raised natives. That is one part by volume each of soil, sand and humus.

For the soil content, a medium loamy type is best, although a heavier or lighter soil can be modified by the addition of extra sand or humus.

The sand can either be fine or coarse, but if you want to be particular, a sharp sand aids the division of heavy roots into finer feeder roots. Bush or river sand is suitable but should be washed to remove silt, as this will hinder the drainage. Make sure that your sand has not been obtained from salty areas.

The humus can be very old compost, leaf mould or aged cow or horse manure for preference, and as a last resort peat moss, if no other humus is available. For more explanation refer to the soil section of our book 'Bonsai in Australia, You Too Can Grow Bonsai'.

Providing you don't allow all the soil to fall away from the root system, the collecting of plants from sandy to light loamy areas, presents no problems when transferred to containerized conditions. This is due to adequate drainage and aeration. Plants from heavy loam to clay areas, will need to have their soil modified to include sand in order to create good drainage which is essential for maintaining healthy conditions in a container.

If a plant is hard to transplant, take some extra soil from the area in which it was growing, and mix with an equal quantity of sand. At the same time, the soil-ball around the trunk should have some of the modified soil introduced into it. This is done by poking some holes with your potting stick into the root-ball and filling with the sandy mix.

Remember, the soil close to the trunk should never be removed, but at each successive potting, more of the sandy mix can be introduced by poking and filling more holes.

A big variation between the original soil around the trunk and the potting mixture, sometimes inhibits the movement of roots into the new soil. Also the rate of drying between the two types of soil can be so uneven, that the heavy area can remain permanently wet, while the sandy section can be bone dry. Another reason for introducing a lighter mix into the soil-ball. Most Australian Natives develop a beneficial fungus around the root-system that enables the nutriments in the soil to be changed into a condition that can be easily absorbed by the feeder roots. This fungus called Mycorrhiza, is usually invisible, nevertheless, without its presence, the plant loses vigour, and slowly starves.

If ideal conditions have been created in the container for the various varieties, i.e. adequate fluctuation from WET to a SLIGHTLY DRY state between waterings, then the Mycorrhiza is able to develop and grow, even though no added Mycorrhiza was introduced.

Conditions that are unfavourable usually are created by inadequate drainage or constantly wet soil. THIS DOES NOT APPLY TO PLANTS THAT NORMALLY GROW IN EITHER DAMP OR SWAMPY AREAS.

Conditions vary in so many areas, that the ideal:— sand, soil and well rotted cow or horse manure often has to be altered to suit its availability and suitability.

In Western Australia for instance, there are only small pockets of what one could consider being called soil. Of what little that can be located ALL falls through a 1/16 th sieve, and is best not used. Another difficulty encountered by the enthusiasts in Perth is that the sand is so fine that it will not accept water. Overhead sprinkling for 10–20 mins. still leaves the centre root-ball bone dry. Immersion for at least 45 mins. is safer but still inadequate.

There is available at some soil & sand merchants crushed granite and sharp crushed river stone. The size to ask for is 1/4 over 1/16th.

Most of the commercially prepared potting mixes in W.A. contain humus comprised of either local or imported peat, jarrah dust, pine bark or sludge, or a combination of the above. These also tend to become water repellant when dry, compounding the problem caused by the fine sand.

If you can buy or collect your own cow or horse manure from a farm be sure to set it aside for at least three months to decompose. This will ensure that the roots are not burnt. Storing in a closed plastic bag or container deprives the manure of oxygen, which is needed if it is to avoid becoming sour. It is only necessary to rub the manure through a coarse sieve to remove the bigger lumps. As W.A. Natives prefer sandy conditions, 50% sand & 50% humus is satisfactory, the main requirement is that the particle size be at least 1/16 th.

In the hot dry atmosphere of W.A. one of the biggest worries is the rapid drying out of the Bonsai. An open porous soil mix in the container actually becomes more filled with water than the finer mixes, thus extending the periods between watering.

Fig. 11 *Poking some holes with potting stick and filling with sandy mix.*

chapter 10

Watering

Many years of work can be lost in a few minutes if your Bonsai is allowed to become bone-dry. Once this has happened, no amount of care and attention can revive it.

On the other hand, (excepting water loving plants) trees that have their soil kept CONSTANTLY wet, will gradually die from the suffocation of the root system.

Few, REALLY, understand the importance of watering and how essential it is to CORRECTLY water any container growing plant. Let us explain it this way. The root system of the plant is like our lungs. Plants breathe through their roots as we through our lungs. To a lesser degree, we also breathe through the pores in our skin. Leaves likewise have pores.

When the plant has been well watered, all the air has been expelled. This becomes very obvious when watering by immersing the container deeper than the level of the pot. Bubbles will rise from the soil, and cease after a few minutes, indicating that the soil is now saturated. The soil then begins to dry out from the surface, both by evaporation, gravity and drainage; the moisture being replaced by air oxygen. The action of this fluctuation between wet to slightly dry is similar to exhaling and inhaling.

To overwater a plant, is not how much water is given at one time but HOW WET THE SOIL IS WHEN REWATERING. Occasionally, we all have to rewater when there is still a lot of moisture left in the soil but this is not harmful to the tree. Six weeks of constant wet conditions, however, depriving the root system of the air, which it also requires, results in the deterioration of the roots. In turn, these are then unable to supply moisture to the top, which strangely enough, produces the same effect as a plant that has died from lack of water.

Constant rain over long periods does no harm, provided adequate drainage and an open porous soil mix has been provided.

chapter 11

Fertilizer

Bonsai Growers tend to differ over the use of fertilizer, some advocating its use, others say it's not necessary. Very often though, all may end with a similar degree of richness.

Some growers start with a rather lean soil, adding fertilizer throughout the growing season, whilst others prepare a rich mixture to start with, and add nothing more.

Although some enthusiasts feed their exotics, they refrain from fertilizing their Natives believing it to be fatal. We start with a medium rich soil mixture, one third of which consists of very old cow manure. When potting, each plant receives some 8–9 month slow release Osmocote or Nutricote at the rate recommended.

We also apply monthly from spring to late autumn, or until the night temps. reach about 15°C an organic fertilizer that we prepare ourselves. It consists of

3 measures soya bean meal
1 measure fish emulsion concentrate
1 measure chicken manure
1 measure blood and bone
1 measure ashes from wood

All the above are placed into a large rubbish bin and covered with water. Do not fill to the top, as it may spill over when fermentation is taking place. Because the water is being absorbed by the mixture as well as evaporation, the mixture needs to be constantly topped up. When the bubbling ceases, water can be added to fill up the bin. It should stand for at least three months. It can either be left in paste form or rolled into balls, or water added and used in liquid form.

The paste is spooned out in teaspoons using about 4 to a 12 cm pot. Similar quantities for the balls. New balls are applied monthly.

For liquid manure, keep the bin filled with added water, and without disturbing the solids at the bottom too much, take about 2 litres of the water and add to a small bucket of water. Dunk your Bonsai once a month.

People in units and those not wishing to go to all the trouble for a few trees may complement the Osmocote or Nutricote, with fish emulsion applied monthly throughout the growing season, at the recommended strength.

Fig. 12 *Paste is spooned out in teaspoons etc.*

In most cases do not use high nitrogenous fertilizers such as Aquasol, Thrive or Zest etc. as this promotes lush growth and long internodes.

Fertilizers containing superphosphate are to be avoided with most Natives, also complete mixtures with a high phosphate rate. With plants requiring an alkaline condition of the soil, you will read that the plant likes lime, but it is safer to obtain dolomite which if used at the correct rate because of its slow release properties is less likely to cause any burning of the roots.

IMPORTANT. Never apply fertilizer to DRY soil. Water well, and then fertilize.

chapter 12

Pruning

Pruning is one of the important techniques for producing Bonsai, but for Natives, correct pruning is essential. Many Australian trees show strong tendencies to grow upwards, often at the expense of the lower branches and any horizontal or drooping growth. With varieties, on which this characteristic occurs, it is important to use pruning to direct vigour in order to create and maintain an acceptable Bonsai form.

Observing many varieties of Eucalypts for instance, this tendency becomes apparent. There is no main truck but many trunk-like branches of similar thickness stretching upwards, constantly shedding sections that have become weakened. This is either because all the strength has been channelled into the more vertical branches, or because of some alteration, for whatever reason, to the position of some of their limbs which results in their deterioration and eventual shedding. The ability to renew itself, especially after fire or drought, is a common characteristic of many Australian trees that can be used to great advantage by the Bonsai enthusiast. If the branches are in the wrong position, — cut them all off, — many shoots will sprout from the trunk, allowing you to select the ones suitable for the style. These shoots should then be left to grow for a season, unpruned, or until the branch has reached the required thickness. Trunks and branches can be drastically shortened, cutting back into bare wood, as long as it is done just prior to regrowth, when the leaf buds are swollen. This is most important. If you cut back to bare wood after the new growth has started, the branch will die back.

If you are pruning back when there is new growth present, make sure you leave at least two pairs of leaves. On the other hand, the renewal characteristic can be even more disastrous for your Bonsai. As explained in the previous chapter, any relaxation of pruning is risky. There exists another problem:— There are many species that sometimes shed their branches when they are positioned below the horizontal, and no amount of pruning back upward growth will help the weakened branch regain its vitality. In most cases, you will find that it keeps shooting from the base of the branch.

chapter 13

Wiring

From the time we first began growing Natives, we had problems when using wire for the shaping of trunks and branches. Some varieties showed adverse reactions by the wired sections either completely dying, becoming dormant or deteriorating back to the highest point in the curve of the branch. Incorrectly believing the problem to be a reaction to copper, we switched to galvanized wire, but the problem persisted, some branches surviving whilst others perished.

Again we changed, this time to aluminium wire, anodized a copper colour, which is much easier to use than any other type, at the same time we were becoming convinced that the type of wire should not be able to influence the vitality of the trunk and branches.

More careful observation indicated that die back occurred only on branches that had developed strong upward growth that had remained untrimmed, or those that had a strong shoot growing from its base, next to the trunk. With this in mind, close attention and constant pruning of all upward growth has proved that any type of wire can be used with safety. What was thought to be a wire problem, turned out to be incorrect or insufficient pruning.

Fig. 13 *Die back occurred only on branches with strong upward growth–A or strong shoot from its base–B.*

chapter 14

The Varieties

Following, is a short list of Australian varieties suitable both horticulturally and artistically for the creation of Bonsai. As with Exotic trees there is a vast range from which to choose. There are many pretty flowering trees, all in proportion both in leaf and flower size. If you prefer Bonsai that have the added attraction of fruit, you will find that these are usually in proportion as well.

Lately, Australian horticulturalists have been concentrating on bringing these plants to the notice of the gardening public, and more and more of these attractive plants are appearing in Nursuries. If your taste is more to the traditional, preferring styles having more of a pine-like appearance, there are a few suitable varieties. However, a well-rounded selection of trees both in the types and variation of material used, as well as many of the styles that are possible, makes a far more interesting collection.

Callistemon
The Bottlebrush

Attraction. The flowers and the colour of the new growth on some varieties. Distinctive bark at an early age.

Suitability for Bonsai. Excellent. Good for the novice.

Choice of material. Suitable for collection. Many varieties available at nurseries, all of them good. Most seed remains in the capsules for a few years, and remains viable. The fine seed is sown in spring. Cuttings can be taken all year especially late summer–autumn.

Transplants well as in most cases there is a fibrous rootsystem. If there is to be major reduction, remove the plant prior to the main growth period in spring.

Rootpruning is done prior to a regrowth period. Although we have slaughtered the roots, we have never bare rooted this variety.

Potting mix. Soil, sand and cow manure with maybe a little extra humus. Neutral to slightly acid.

Fertilizer is necessary.

Styles. All styles, no weakening of branches below the horizontal.

Pruning. Cut into bare wood prior to regrowth. Prune back below the old flowers.

Trimming. Allow the spring growth to extend until the flowers appear. Keep the Bonsai tidy by trimming the shoots extending past the flower buds. At all other times pinch out the new tips leaving only a few leaves.

Wiring no problem.

Watering. Most varieties appreciate moist conditions. Can use a shallow water tray in summer.

Location. Plenty of light is necessary to induce flowering. Some are frost tender.

Acacias
The Wattles

Attraction. A very familiar tree even to non gardeners. A symbol of Australia. Yellow fluffy balls of flowers.

Suitability for Bonsai is generally good, depending on the variety. It has a reputation as being a short lived tree, but with good soil and correct watering and attention to pests, it has the potential to live longer as a Bonsai.

Varieties. As there is in excess of 400 varieties, your choice will be determined by local varieties that can be collected, or those obtainable from a nursery. Acacia foliage can either look feathery, called bipinnate — example, Cootamundra Wattle. Or as the Sydney Golden Wattle which has the type called phyllodes, being more 'leaf like'. Some varieties produce both types on the same tree which especially on the smaller Bonsai tend to look untidy. Larger Bonsai, depending on the style can look reasonably presentable with both the juvenile and mature foliage present at the same time.

A. glaucescens, the Coast Myall having phyllodes is one of the best.
A. longifolia, the Sydney Golden Wattle, has phyllodes and is hardy.
A. mollissima, the Black Wattle, bipinnate leaves.
A. podalyriifolia, Qld. Silver Wattle, phyllodes.
The above are a few that we have found hardy.

Seed holds its viability for many years and is VERY hard. It must be softened before it will germinate. This is done by scarifying the outer coat, i.e. rubbing with sandpaper, by applying heat in a dry form, i.e. in the ashes of a fire, or with boiling water, allowing it to soak for an hour or two and sowing immediately, late summer being a good time. Not all varieties strike from cuttings.

Transplants from self sown stock with difficulty as the tap root is very long, with no feeder roots close to the trunk. When unearthing this root it can often be mistaken for a sucker. If the beauty of a particular plant warrants its removal, preparation of the root system is required.

Rootpruning is no problem once a fibrous root system has been obtained, or from cultivated stock. Acacia roots supply nitrogen to the soil via the bacteria that develops in association with the rootsystem. The nodules that are present on the roots are an indication of this phenomenon and are not a disease. It is also an indication that the rootsystem is hardy and can withstand rootpruning. Can be bare rooted, although if your soil is satisfactory no need to remove more than the outer third of the soil-ball.

Potting mix. Sand, soil and cow manure, irrespective of variety.

Fertilizer. The same as the other species.

Styles. Upright styles are better, a slight loss of vigour with cascades.

Pruning revitalizes this species which can be reduced to bare wood at rootpruning time which can be anytime before regrowth. At other times leave some foliage present.

Trimming is constant through the growing period. Trim back each time to the first or second leaf depending on direction. With the elongation of the spring growth will come the flowers, so retain the length necessary for the flowers and then pinch out the tip. After flowering, cut hard back. The varieties with bipinnate leaves can be kept tidier by trimming back, leaving a few pairs of 'leaves' on each stem. (Illustration with Grevillea robusta.)

Wiring is safe as long as the upward growth is checked.

Watering. Usual watering for most varieties as long as good drainage has been provided. Even though our glaucescens was obtained from a sandbar in the river, giving it a water tray or keeping it on the dry side has not produced any variation in its appearance.

Location. Seems to stand light frost, and coastal conditions.

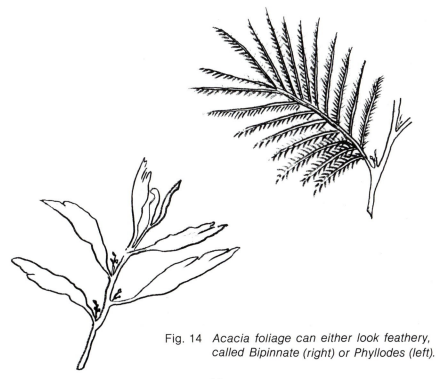

Fig. 14 *Acacia foliage can either look feathery, called Bipinnate (right) or Phyllodes (left).*

Ceratopetalum gummiferum
N.S.W. Christmas Bush

Attraction. Small white flowers with the calyx turning red about Christmas time.

Choice of material. Most enthusiasts start from nursery stock, although quite large plants from gardens or countryside can be successfully removed. Cuttings are very unreliable for the home gardener.

The seed should be collected when it has ripened, late summer (Jan.–Feb.) and sown immediately. They can be grafted, but the only reason would be to obtain a rich red colour. This would be done in spring, before the scion (piece to be grafted) starts to grow.

Transplants fairly well if the collected plant has been growing in a moist loamy soil as the root system will be more compact. The best time is either just prior to the spring regrowth or late summer (January) as soon as the 'flowers' have finished.

Rootpruning is tolerated as long as the roots close to the trunk are not disturbed. Do not bare root. Although spring is a good time, we usually rootprune late summer (January) just as it is about to reshoot.

Potting mix. Light loamy soil, sand and cow manure in equal quantities, with the emphasis on GOOD drainage. It is generally known that in their natural habitat they like moisture. In a container, if kept constantly wet, they will deteriorate.

Fertilizer. Osmocote or Nutricote at potting time. Our 'paste' at monthly intervals, or B&B and fish emulsion substituted. To improve the colour of the calyx, ½ teaspoon per medium pot of iron sulphate should be sprinkled on the soil and watered in. This is best applied in spring.

Styles. Informal uprights seem to be the most suitable style. Some weakening occurred with cascades.

Pruning. Never cut back to hard bare wood. Very slow to shoot on old wood. If reduction is necessary leave one or two pairs of leaves, fertilize well and hope. The best pruning time is after flowering.

Trimming. If your major pruning and shaping is done in summer (January), only light trimming is necessary to keep your Bonsai tidy. Do not trim after the spring growth if you want flowers.

Wiring. Only just tolerates wire. Have noticed that although not dying, branches seem to be less vigorous. Wood is brittle, hard to bend and takes a long time to 'set'.

Watering. Usual watering all year, but they like plenty of water in summer as long as the drainage is good.

Location. Can stand sun all year but should be sheltered from scorching sun in mid-summer. Frost tender.

Fig. 15 *Large plants from gardens or countryside can be cut down and successfully removed.*

Eugenia, Acmena or Syzygium
Lillypilly and Brush cherry

Attraction. Cream fluffy flowers, purple to white fruit, glossy leaves.

Suitability for Bonsai is excellent. Extremely good material for the novice to gain experience.

Choice of material. Cuttings can be taken in winter, using older wood. Summer cuttings use the spring growth that has slightly matured and must be kept humid either under glass or plastic. Seeds must be collected when ripe in autumn and not allowed to become dry. They do not have long viability so it is better to sow immediately and keep slightly moist until spring when they should germinate quickly. Collecting old trees from gardens or countryside is possible. Aerial layering by removing sections of the bark works better than complete ringbarking, but nursery stock is the most popular method.

Transplants as easily as most deciduous exotics.

Rootpruning is best done in spring, August in most areas, before the new growth appears. It is also possible at any other time when the leaves have hardened and the tree has been dormant for a while, and the leaf buds look as if they will soon start sprouting. We have never bare rooted any of this group, but at times the root system has been considerably reduced with no ill effects.

Soil. Sand, loamy soil and cow manure with a little extra humus. Slightly acid.

Fertilizer. They respond very well to fertilizing, and definitely require extra nutriment to encourage flowers and fruit. At potting time osmocote or nutricote. A few weeks later Phostrogen can be sprinkled on the surface of the soil and watered in. This is for the flowers and fruit. It can be applied monthly, but is especially useful in autumn. We also use our 'paste, but B&B and fish emulsion can be substituted.

Styles. Suitable for all styles. No loss of vigour with cascades.

Pruning. Shoots back from bare wood. We usually leaf prune each year at potting time especially if the leaves have become damaged by scale, gall wasps or leaf hoppers. Never remove the leaves more than once a year, and then only if the plant has been fertilized and is in a healthy condition.

Trimming. As the internodes are rather long, cut back to the basic shape when repotting and allow to grow untrimmed until the start of next season's growth when it is again trimmed to the first set of leaves. As the flowers develop on the new growth, the Bonsai remains presentable at all times.

Wiring is not a problem although care should be taken when bending as the wood is rather brittle.

Watering should not be neglected as it is a waterloving plant, but GOOD drainage is essential so there can be a more constant rewatering pattern.

Location. From semi shade to full sun. Can stand slight frosts. Can tolerate salty conditions as long as the leaves are sometimes washed clean.

Fig. 16 *Lilly Pilly seedlings were twisted together when young and as they increased in size – became welded together forming a thicker trunk.*

Rulingia hermanifolia

This is a very showy plant, and because of its ease of transplanting makes it a very desirable addition to the native collection. The profusion of small pink flowers are at their peak around the middle of September, and remain attractive for several weeks until the flowers become brown. Shortly afterwards, small round seed capsules become evident adding more interest to your Bonsai.

Suitability for Bonsai is excellent; small leaves and flowers will produce a well proportioned Bonsai.

Choice of material is mainly nursery stock, although cuttings 'take' very well, and if grown in a big tub or in the ground, a reasonably large plant can be produced in a year.

Transplants very well, either by bare rooting or removing the outer root ball only.

Rootpruning can be done as the flower buds are becoming prominent; this is usually about the beginning of August. At this time, do not trim the ends where the buds are if you wish to enjoy the flowers. In many cases, the length of the trunk or branch *can* be shortened, as there is usually an abundance of side shoots, with flowers, which will still provide a spectacular display. We usually do our rootpruning after flowering, at which time the plant is severely pruned back.

Soil. Sand, soil and cow manure in equal quantities.

Fertilizer. At potting time, Osmocote or nutricote is applied as the soil mix is being added to the pot. About one month later we start applying our organic 'paste' at monthly intervals until the middle of summer, and resume in February, or early March and continue until the night temps. drop to about 18°C. If unable to make the paste, use blood & bone, about 1 teaspoon per medium sized pot (22 cm or 9 in.) applied to a wet surface, twice in spring and autumn. Fish emulsion can be applied at the same time. Directions are on the bottle.

Styles. Any style is possible with Rulingia. Especially miniatures.

Pruning. This plant can be pruned back even into bare wood, and reshoot well. This should only be done though, at rootpruning time, or prior to the time of regrowth. Light pruning is safe at any time other than early to mid winter.

Trimming. Unless lengthening the branches, the new shoots should be kept trimmed to one or two new leaves. The side shoots develop so rapidly, that a well ramified branch can be obtained in one year. By autumn (April or May depending how cold it gets in your area) the plant should be trimmed so that it looks tidy. In late winter–early spring (August) the buds will appear at the ends of the sub branches in such profusion giving the appearance of clouds.

Wiring is no problem; the wood is very pliable and can stand acute changes of angles. It tolerates any type of wire.

Watering. No special or different watering requirements are necessary.

Location. Takes shade or sun. Seems to be frost hardy.

Fig. 17 *Rulingia*

Banksia

Attraction. The aged gnarled trunks of the Old Man Banksia.

Suitability for Bonsai is good, although some varieties are harder to develop into and maintain a trim Bonsai shape.

Choice of material. The varieties we have used are ericifolia, integrifolia, marginata, spinulosa and the best one being serrata, the Old Man Banksia for its marvellous swelling of the trunk. Nursery stock is the most common material used, although people close to a collecting area can save a lot of time by digging out larger plants. Some varieties strike from cuttings. Ericifolia, for instance can develop an interesting base of trunk, still, as with most species, the best bases develop on plants produced from seed. The Banksia seed is very hard and needs to be soaked in water for about a week, then dried very quickly either in the sun or over heat.

Transplants well. After bushfires is a good time to collect large specimens, especially of serrata; at other times only when no new shoots are present, then defoliate.

Rootpruning. When collecting varieties with the tuber-like base that has had everything burned back to the tuber, cut back or defoliated, the rootsystem can be bare rooted or cut drastically. With future repotting, no need to bare root. The timing can be anytime prior to regrowth.

Soil. Sand, sandy loam and cow manure in equal quantities. Acid conditions. Good drainage is absolutely essential.

Fertilizer. They respond well to our 'paste', light application of B&B and, or fish emulsion once a month when the plant is growing. Osmocote or nutricote at potting time.

Styles. B. ericifolia, because of its small leaves, fine shoots and its branching habit is the most traditional material of the species. B. serrata can very easily look like a potted oddity if its tuber is allowed to develop into a potato like form, so it is important to select a shoot and continue a tapering trunkline. Do not allow too many branches to grow around the area where the trunk and tuber meet as their presence helps to increase the diameter of the tuber at the point where it should be slimmer. If this is attended to, then serrata can be used for any of the styles.

Fig. 18 *B. serrata can look like a potted oddity if its tuber is allowed to develop into a potato like form.*

Fig. 19 *Select a shoot and continue a tapering trunkline.*

Pruning can be drastic on all varieties; they reshoot well but is safer just at the end of a dormant period.

Trimming by pinching the new shoots, or cutting back when slightly matured on ericifolia, spinulosa and serrata. Integrifolia and marginata have a more awkward pattern of growth. There is long internodal space with alternate leaves between 'whorl-like' buds. To keep your Bonsai compact the new shoots must be pulled out before they have a chance to stretch.

Wiring is acceptable to this species, and because the wood is pliable, extreme bending is possible. No loss of vigour from bending below the horizontal.

Watering. As long as the Banksias are not kept in a waterlogged condition, your usual watering pattern suits them.

Location. Most varieties can stand coastal conditions, also the above are not frost tender.

Casuarina
She Oak, Australian Pine

Attraction. Their Pine like appearance.

Suitability for Bonsai. Excellent, should be more widely used and become one of the most important species for Bonsai in Australia. In Hawaii, this species is as impressive as the Japanese Black pine.

Choice of material. C. cunninghamiana, River She Oak is no. 1 variety and is the easiest to remove from its habitat. Growing in or close to fresh water ensures a compact root mass. C. torulosa, the Forest She Oak would be a close rival to the former, not because of its ease of removal from the 'wild', but for its attractive corky bark. As this variety usually grows in drier situations, it is not as easy to remove in one operation as cunninghamiana. C. glauca, the Swamp oak, as its name suggests also grows in wet areas, and is therefore easy to remove. C. stricta, the Drooping She Oak is another forest tree, and also requires more care for successful removal.

There are many more varieties, but the above are the ones we have used.

Casuarinas strike from cuttings quite easily, but more success will be obtained in autumn with semi mature wood. The seeds are produced in cone like fruit, collected when they have opened, and sown in spring. This species can be grafted, but possibly the only reason for doing so, would be to graft a finer 'foliaged' variety onto an impressive trunk of a coarser foliaged plant. It can also be aerial layered.

Transplants easily in some cases, more difficult with others from the 'wild' as described previously. Because these roots attract nitrogen producing bacteria which is evident by tiny nodules on the roots, the operation of rootpruning is less of a trauma.

Rootpruning is best done in spring or autumn when the plant is just about to shoot. Treat as a conifer and never remove the main area of soil around the trunk.

Potting mix. The basic sand, soil and cow manure is suitable for all varieties with some modification — the wet area plants can receive more humus, whilst the drier varieties should be given more sand. All varieties require acid conditions, but the 'wet ones' will develop more acidity due to their excessive water requirements.

Fertilizer is necessary to encourage constant reshooting as is explained under pruning. Our 'paste' or B&B and/or fish emulsion should be applied monthly during the growing period. Osmocote or nutricote at potting time.

Styles. All styles are possible, only a slight weakening of branches and foliage at the end of cascades which can be expected with upright trees, however, correct pruning can overcome this problem.

Pruning for drastic reduction is possible, as well as cutting back to bare wood. Complete defoliation is also safe as long as all are done prior to regrowth. If position of branches can be improved — cut them all off and start again. Like the Eucalypts, so many shoots develop along the trunk that at times you are forever having to rub them off. Allow the bottom branches to grow untrimmed at the ends until the required thickness is obtained. Remember though, any branchlets growing strongly upwards must be trimmed or removed, otherwise die-back will occur along the end of your elongating branch to the point of the upward growth.

When you are fairly satisfied with the trunk, branches and sub-branches, all other growth should be removed each year prior to the strongest growing period; that way all growth is completely renewed each year.

Trimming is a constant task during all growing periods. The 'needles' on most varieties are rather long and need to be shortened. This is easy to do with casuarinas. Each 'needle' is in fact a stalk and the microscopic foliage is at the little serrations between the sections. These come apart when pulled and do not become brown as is the case when scissors are used.

Wiring is safe as long as no shoots are allowed to develop too strongly vertically either from the base of the branch or along it. The wood takes a long time to 'set'.

Watering varies with the variety. The river oak can sit in a SHALLOW tray of water in summer, but if it does not completely evaporate daily, flush it out and replace with fresh water. C. glauca is the contrary. As its requirements need brackish water, a deeper tray can be kept topped up. The other two varieties listed should have extra sand in the potting mix, so they can be watered with your other Bonsai, but they will become slightly drier, which are the conditions they need to thrive.

Location close to the sea will not harm them. Frost hardy.

Lagunaria Pattersoni
Norfolk Island hibiscus, Cow-Itch tree

Attraction. Rosy pink flowers followed by large reddish seeds.

Suitability for Bonsai. An excellent tree for the novice.

Choice of material. As there are only two or three areas where they grow naturally, Lord Howe and Norfolk Islands and a small area in Queensland, the chances of collecting are slim. However, they can be transplanted with ease as fairly large specimens both from the 'wild' and the garden. The seed has a high viability rate and should be planted in spring. Be careful when handling the seed as the short, stiff hairs produce a painful itch. It also reproduces from cuttings.

Transplants with ease.

Rootpruning. At anytime between regrowth. Can be bare rooted.

Potting mix. Sand, any type of soil between sandy and loamy, and cow manure in equal quantities. Adaptable to acid or alkaline conditions.

Fertilizer. Osmocote or Nutricote at potting time. A week or two later Phostrogen is added and watered in, then a month or two later we start applying our 'paste', but fish emulsion can be substituted.

Styles. All styles; no loss of vigour with cascades.

Pruning. Can stand hard pruning to bare wood at repotting time. As leaves are often eaten by leaf hoppers, partial defoliation is safe during the growing period, and any large leaves that develop are removed. We usually totally defoliate at potting time and this helps to study the form and apply new wire with ease.

Trimming. Unless extending the height or width, pinch young tips before they elongate too much, in order to reduce the internodal length.

Wiring is not a problem. Trunk and branches are easy to bend.

Watering. They are very adaptable; moderate overwatering or underwatering does not affect them.

Location. They are not affected by salt spray. Can stand slight frost.

Leptospermum
The Tea-Tree

Attraction. Small flowers and fine foliage. Beautiful bark.

Suitability for Bonsai is variable. Seems to be determined by the variety. The size of the flowers and foliage are ideal.

Varieties. The most irresistible varieties are those derived from L. scoparium. They have minute leaves and white to red flowers. Unfortunately, they are very touchy. We have rootpruned them at all times of the year to no avail. We have singed the leaves without success. It seems that to touch the roots is to ask for trouble, as the only time we have succeeded was by planting 3 small plants into a Saikei (landscape with rock) and waited for them to grow and develop. L. flavescens, the Common Tea-Tree. L. laevigatum, the Coastal Tea-Tree an, L. petersonii, the Lemon Scented Tea-Tree, L. attenuatum and L. flavens nana are all worth trying.

The hybrids from L. scoparium can only be propagated from cuttings taken from late summer to winter. The species varieties are developed from fine seed enclosed in capsules. As these begin to ripen they should be collected and placed in a paper bag as the capsule can open rather quickly and the seed is scattered. Sow in spring.

Transplants with some success other than scoparium. With L. attenuatum, we found the initial removal from its natural habitat had to be accompanied with the removal of the leaves. This was done by singeing. We found it was not necessary with repotting.

Rootpruning. Only about one third of the roots are removed. Never bare root.

Potting mix. Well draining mixture of sand, soil and humus. Acid.

Fertilizer. As the other species.

Styles. All styles, including cascade.

Pruning. Can stand severe pruning, reshoots well. Cut into bare wood prior to regrowth only.

Trimming is constant. Either pull the ends of new growth or trim with scissors after some elongation has occurred.

Wiring is possible. New wood is pliable; older wood is more brittle.

Watering. In nature the varieties vary with their needs for water. Under cultivation treat all the same as any other Bonsai.

Location. Salt tolerant. All can stand a light frost only.

Podocarpus

The Plum Pine, P. elatus and its smaller brother, P. alpinus or Lawrencii as it is sometimes named are both good specimens for Bonsai, with the latter being more suitable for miniatures because of its finer foliage.

Very evident on the roots of all podocarps are the nitrogen fixing nodules. Rootpruning, therefore is very safe. Cultivation is similar to Callistemon. Strikes from cuttings at any time. The nut seed should be collected when ripe and sown immediately. Aerial layers best in spring.

Fig. 20   *Nitrogen nodules on roots.*

Dacrydium franklinii
Huon Pine

Shape your Huon Pine in such a way that it will show to advantage, the thread like pendulous branchlets in much the same way as a willow. A more classical appearance will be achieved by pulling out the new shoots when they reach the desired length. Sometimes you may notice deterioration from this trimming, and so decide to allow the branchlets to droop. They stand wiring but the wood is very pliable and takes a long time to become set in position. The usual soil mix and 'normal' watering, repotting in spring.

Propagated from seed and strikes easily from cutting, but as the branchlets are long and limp, they will need to have a deep pot of sand, inserting the heel into the hole as deep as possible.

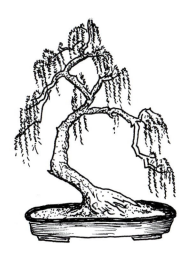

Fig. 21   *A suitable style.*

Tristania conferta
Brush Box

Related to the Eucalypts and possessing a lignotuber at the base that develops into an attractive buttress, beautiful bark, and the ability to reshoot from the trunk should make this variety desirable Bonsai material. Unfortunately, the branching is rather coarse, and the internodes a little too long. Its worst problem is it resents trimming. If unmatured growth is trimmed, the branch will probably die back. Hard pruning is acceptable late winter and late summer when there is no soft growth on the tree. The better way to style a presentable conferta, is to concentrate on obtaining an attractive trunkline, with a few well placed branches which will be cut back hard each year to a point close to the trunk. The elongating shoots are then left to grow untrimmed.

Fig. 22B *When leaves mature, cut off leaves.*

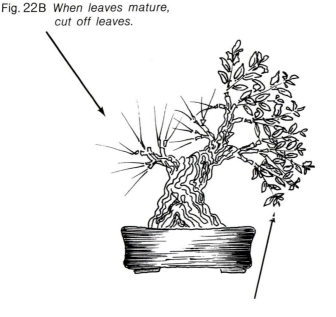

Fig. 22A *Shoots are left to grow untrimmed.*

When this growth has matured, and there is no young foliage on the tree, the leaves can be cut off, (defoliated) and the branch shortened. This would take place in summer. Stands rootpruning, but don't bare root. Likes moisture.

T. laurina, the Water Gum is not as difficult to work with. It can stand in a shallow water tray in summer.

Tristania are propagated from seed that can be sown at any time.

Fig. 23 *Attractive trunkline; few well placed branches*
— cut back hard each year.

Microstrobos

There are two species of this conifer, one from New South Wales, M. fitzgeraldi, the other is from Tasmania, M. niphophilis. They are both water loving plants and reasonably tolerant of container growing, although fitzgeraldi is possibly the more hardy of the two. They are most attractive when planted on the rock, but great care must be taken to ensure that they are not allowed to become too dry.

Its styling would be similar to the Huon Pine which belongs also to this genus, but as it is a more shrub-like plant, makes it excellent material for miniatures. Treat them as conifers and never bare the roots close to the trunk. The usual soil mix, with perhaps a little more humus. It is safer to repot in spring as the new growth is about to appear. Very often sections of the pendulous growth seem to be dead, but eventually green shoots will begin to grow from it.

Fig. 24 *They are most attractive when planted on rock.*

Colour Plates

chapter

Tea Tree.
Leptospermum attenuatum.
Height: 43 cm.

Our first attempts to transplant this variety of Leptospermum were unsuccessful despite great care at various times of the year. The beautiful flaky bark induced us to keep trying, and finally in 1968 after removing all the leaves when transplanting, this tree survived. It was kept as a miniature until 1978 when it was planted into a larger pot to start increasing its size. Plans for the future include the tilting of the trunk to a more vertical position, removal of the lower right hand branches and the trunk about 6 cm above the first left branch, redirecting the trunk towards the left. See diagram.

Port Jackson Fig.
Ficus rubiginosa.
Height: 47 cm.

Collected in 1976 as an upright tree, the trunk was sawn across about 20 cm from the ground. A V-shaped wedge was carved out and the trunk tilted so that the left side of the wedge was in a horizontal position. By doing this, the branchlets that would grow around the edge of the carving would help to give it the appearance of a branch. (See the enlargement.)

At the same time, heavy right hand roots were cut out and some aerial roots tied close to the trunk and covered with sphagnum to encourage their thickening. Many shoots grew around the edge of the cut, so they were grafted and welded together to make more rugged looking branches. The same was done to the branches at the top of the cut so they would form a more substantial trunk.

Coast Myall.
Acacia glaucescens.
Height: 80 cm.

One of the original trees collected from the Nepean River in 1956. The three major roots of this Wattle were clasping a round river stone. Until shortly before this photograph was taken, these exposed roots were emphasized by planting in a shallow container. The decision to change the appearance of the Bonsai, meant its planting into a deep pot, and filling in the space between the roots. The photograph was taken in autumn, showing the growth that has occurred since spring, when the tree was severely pruned.

White Cloud Tree.
Melaleuca bracteata.
Height: 66 cm.

From tubed nursery stock bought in 1968. It was planted at the side of an attractive trunk of a paper bark found in the bush. By 1979, the old trunk had rotted away, but the plant had become presentable enough without it.

Lilly Pilly.
Eugenia smithii.
Height: 68 cm.

This Bonsai was started from seed collected by us in 1966. The photograph was taken as the autumn growth was beginning to appear. Fruit also hangs on the tree. The stoneware pot, by Vita Koreshoff was made in ancient Chinese style.

Blueberry Ash.
Eleocarpus reticulatus Pink.
Height: 70 cm.
The two main trees were started from nursery stock in 1966. The three smaller plants were cuttings taken from the original trees in 1972. The group was assembled in 1975.

Heath Banksia.
Banksia ericifolia.
Height: 50 cm.
A small plant bought in 1968, was kept as a miniature mainly because of its tiny leaves. About 1975 it was planted into a larger pot to increase the size. It was potted into the pictured container which is a stoneware pot by Vita Koreshoff, in 1980, and two years later, during extensive restyling, several old, large lower branches were removed and the apex extended. The picture was taken 6 weeks after rootpruning and trimming back the branches.

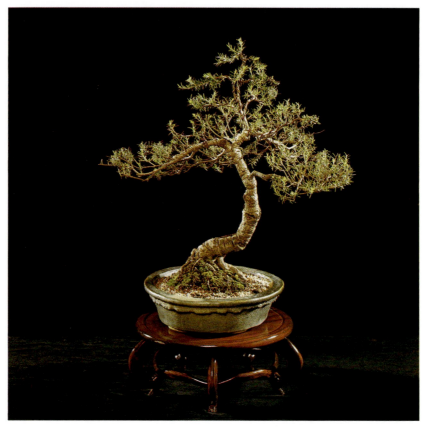

Bottlebrush.
Callistemon 'Captain Cook'.
Height: 64 cm.
Originated from advanced nursery stock in 1970. The picture was taken in autumn as new shoots are developing. It was severely pruned after flowering and will be lightly trimmed in late autumn.

Paperbark.
Melaleuca decussata.
Height: 58 cm.

In 1975, observing a fantastic paperbark with mauve flowers growing next to a lake in Disneyland was the incentive to send us in search of advanced material of the same variety. The two trees chosen for the setting had trunks of similar diameter, but one had a small trunk towards the rear that could be used to give the illusion of greater width. Each year, the fine twigs are shortened back to the heavier branches prior to a growing period, and finger tipped pruned to obtain a trim shape. Often, when short of time, the foliage is trimmed with scissors as if pruning a hedge. The photograph was taken in autumn with the twigs about 12 months old showing a typical characteristic of some natives to shed the lower leaves thus showing a mass of very fine branchlets with foliage only on the ends.

She Oak.
Casuarina cunninghamiana.
Height: 80 cm.
One of several She Oaks collected from the banks of the Nepean River in April 1956. This tree appeared to have been severely damaged by floodwater, for the top had been broken off and the trunk split in half vertically. The growth of the past 27 years has resulted in the gradual encirclement of the driftwood down the front, and the formation of a new head.

Old Man Banksia.
Banksia serrata.
Height: 36 cm.

This Banksia was collected at a Bonsai Club dig in 1968. Not long before, a bushfire had swept through the area charring many plants. This Banksia had lost its branches and all that remained was a blackened tuber. Confident the plant would survive after removal in this burnt condition, it was planted into a large training pot for two years while the new branches developed. It was eventually planted into a Bonsai pot not much larger than the tuber, and for many years remained more of an oddity than a Bonsai. In 1978 some large roots were removed from the right side and the tuber turned to a slanting position. (Note the folds in a more vertical position.) For the photograph, a long branch about 8 cm above the tuber, used for the thickening of that section of the trunk, was removed.

Port Jackson Fig.
Ficus rubiginosa.
Height: 63 cm.

This Fig, growing in a 12 gallon drum, was purchased from a nursery in 1949. Removal from the tin exposed a long L-shaped trunk reaching to the bottom of the container. As it was, the material was unsuitable, so the decision to cut the trunk in two resulted in branches developing on the bottom section, (pictured) and roots on the upper portion, thus gaining two trees. We call this our walking Fig. Note the mass of aerial roots to the left of the trunk. The picture was taken about 6 weeks after complete defoliation, repotting and rewiring.

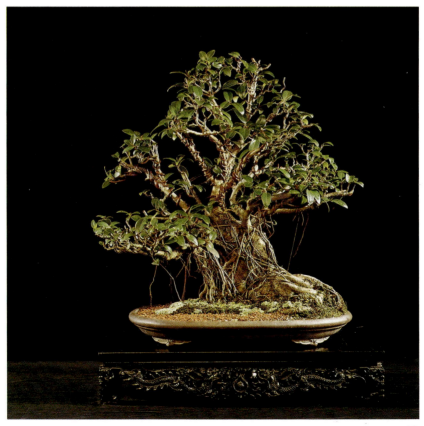

Gum Tree.
Eucalyptus.
Height: 53 cm.

Since 1963 this tree has undergone a lot of experiment and trials. It is one of the lucky Eucalypts that survived. The picture shows that Eucalypts can be wired and styled as any other plants, as long as correct pruning is observed. The picture was taken in autumn after late summer pruning, which removed all the foliage and shortened all branches. The main growing period has just started and by spring the branches will have lengthened and multiplied, the apex kept to its present size, and the overall shape, rounded, giving a softer appearance.

Melia azedarach
White Cedar

A deciduous tree with beautiful mauve flowers followed by hard bead like fruit. The roots and trunk are attractive, but, like the Brachychiton, the top leaves a lot to be desired. It is extremely hardy and can stand slaughtering of the roots and top, provided it is done prior to regrowth in spring. Treat as any other deciduous tree.

Cuphea alba
White Cigar Flower

This little shrub is very useful as a miniature as it not only resembles the Serissa, but is as easy to cultivate and shape. Can be rootpruned at any time when there is no new growth present. There are other colours which are just as hardy, but the white is the most attractive.

Callitris
Cypress Pine

The fine cypress type foliage of this Australian conifer presents to the Bonsaist, material that can well be called traditional. It should be transplanted carefully from the countryside, as it is usually found growing in dry locations. Try to keep as much of the soil close to the trunk as possible, although sometimes this can be difficult if growing in sandy soil. Mycorrhiza is important to this species. It can stand very hard pruning, which is very desirable especially if the root system has been reduced drastically when transplanting. We have found the best time for this is summer, when the tree is dormant. Make SURE there is no new growth present otherwise you are likely to be unsuccessful. Trimming should continue during the growing period by pulling out the ends which will come apart between the scales without browning. Responds to wiring, and the wood, being fairly pliable when young takes some time to 'set'. Prefers to be kept more on the dry side, so extra sand in the soil mix will allow this to occur more quickly.

Propagates from seed or cutting.

Eleocarpus reticulatus
Blueberry Ash

Withstands drastic rootpruning, pruning, wiring and trimming, but its method of growth is awkward, the internodes long, and the wood is rather brittle and difficult to acutely change the shape. These failings can often be disguised by planting as a group.

The plant is better shaped when young and developed fast, or find a very large tree that can be cut down. Unfortunately, the trunk tends to still be slender even with age. It is mostly admired for the white or pink flowers and the berries. Leaf size can be reduced by defoliation in summer. The seed is collected when ripe in spring, allowed to ferment a few days in water, and sown immediately. The seed should not be allowed to dry before sowing. Slow to germinate. A more interesting base is obtained from seed. They strike from cutting, but the trunk is more pole like.

Grevillea robusta
Silky Oak

Owing to the compound formation of the leaves, a true Bonsai-like appearance is hard to achieve. One way to do it would be to trim back several sections of the 'leaves' giving the branches a more compact effect. Their cultivation is suitable for the novice, as it accepts rootpruning, wiring, pruning and plenty of sun without deterioration. Hard pruning and repotting should be done prior to regrowth in either spring or autumn. Acid conditions. Good drainage. Seed is sown in spring.

Fig. 25 *Light section shows where 'leaf' can be trimmed to reduce overall size and obtain a more tidy appearance.*

Grevillea
Various Varieties

Many of the varieties, especially some cultivars are suitable for cascading. Be careful to arch the trunk out of the pot, and not allow them to lay over the top of the container. If planting in a cascade pot make sure that there is extra sand in the mix, which should be very open. Grevillea, although requiring acid conditions, deteriorate very quickly if kept constantly moist. The finer foliaged type rosmarinifolia are more suitable for the upright styles, leaving the ground cover types for cascades. Prefers sunny position. Short cuttings with heels late summer–winter. Suitable and possible to graft onto stock of robusta in spring. Seed, if applicable, is sown in spring.

Fig. 26 *Arch the trunk out of the pot.*

Fig. 27 *Not to lay over the top of pot.*

45

Araucaria bidwillii.
Bunya Pine

Responds well to container growing. Rootprunes with ease before a growing period. Its growth and foliage pattern makes it hard to conform to what is regarded as suitable traditional type material. We persevered for years dissatisfied with its appearance, so cut it back to the thick buttress and turned it into an 'interesting' semi cascade. ALL strong upward growth is removed leaving only selected weak cascading branches.

Fig. 28 *After being cut back to the thick buttress, it turned into an 'interesting' semi cascade.*

Brachychiton

Includes the Illawarra Flame tree, Lacebark, Kurrajong, Bottle Tree. All have interesting roots and trunks, but the top is more pot plant like than Bonsai, owing to fewer, coarser branches and type of leaves. As it likes dry conditions during the winter, it is safer to include at least 50% sand in the potting mix. Likes lime. Cut back into bare wood each year at potting time which will be late spring, October or November. If you cut below foliage at any other time the branch or trunk will die back. They are nearly all deciduous, depending where it is growing. Grown from seed in a container, the strong tap-root twists and turns producing a wide contorted buttress. These roots can be reduced drastically, not necessarily leaving any fibrous roots, as the trunk has enough stored moisture and nutriments and is able to sustain the plant for long periods.

Fig. 29 *Interesting root and trunk top, more like pot plant.*

Varieties in Brief

Agonis flexuosa, Willow Myrtle

Cultivation similar to Callistemon. Seed easily raised in spring.

Albizzia lophantha, Cape Wattle

Cultivation similar to Acacia. Excellent roots and trunk but compound leaves.

Hakea Varieties

Cultivation similar to Callistemon. Seed and cuttings in spring and autumn.

Hymenosporum flavum, Native Frangipanni

Cultivation similar to Callistemon. Seed is sown late summer to autumn.

Kunzea ambigua & baxteri.

Cultivation similar to Callistemon. Seed sown in spring. Cuttings in autumn.

Melaleuca, Paperbarks.

Cultivation similar to Callistemon. Seed is sown in spring. Cuttings summer–winter.

Pittosporum Varieties

Cultivation similar to Lilly Pilly. Species sown by seed when ripe. Cuttings autumn–winter.

Eucalypts & Angophora

One of the most common questions asked is 'Can you Bonsai a Gum'? More interest and awe surrounds this species than any other Native, but providing you follow a slightly different procedure to the 'normal', the answer is yes.

Choice of material is mainly nursery stock and collecting. The seed capsules can be collected and stored until required. The seed remains viable for many years. As most of the seed is rather fine, it may be difficult to separate from the rubbish, but sow altogether in spring with only a light covering of whatever humus you use. Viable seed should sprout in only a few weeks. Separate the seedlings as soon as they are big enough to handle, and cut the taproot. Plant into a training pot with plenty of nitrogenous fertilizer, shape the trunk, at the same time try to develop a thick trunk by allowing as much growth to extend without trimming. All branches should be removed and the trunk shortened to the required height when the trunk has thickened sufficiently. The plant is again rootpruned and returned to the training pot for another year to develop the branches. Masses of shoots will grow from the trunk. Select branches for the correct positions and rub off all the others. The bottom branches on a Bonsai should be the thickest, so allow those to grow untrimmed until the required thickness has been obtained, remembering to remove any growth close to the base of the branch. Remove any vertical shoots along the branch. Only immature growth can be used for cuttings and then only a poor percentage will take root.

We have obtained more success with E. saligna, (Sydney Blue Gum); E. nicholii, (Peppermint Gum); E. maculata, (Spotted Gum); and E. sideroxylon, (Pink Flowering Ironbark).

The variety you choose must have the ability to branch close to the ground, as the role for some is to provide a tall canopy to shade the undergrowth. If, after several prunings your tree still has not branched, discard it as it is not suitable for Bonsai.

Transplants with reasonable safety, if ALL the leaves are removed either by cutting or singeing over a fire. The flame should only be hot enough to dry out the leaves but not destroy the branches. In a day or two the leaves will fall naturally.

Some Eucalypts, along with a few other species, produce a swelling starting either under or above the soil around the base of the trunk,

Fig.30   *Produce a swelling starting either under or above
the soil — called a lignotuber.*

called a lignotuber. This is made up of undifferentiated cells, which, depending on the conditions surrounding a particular part of the tuber, have the ability to either produce branches or roots. One of the important factors ensuring successful rootpruning is, UNDER NO CIRCUMSTANCES should the roots, trunk or lignotuber be planted deeper than the original level of the soil, otherwise the tree will surely die. There is no danger from exposing MORE of the tuber or root.

Rootpruning time differs from exotics, for the Eucalypts grow throughout the winter in most areas above freezing point. They still have fresh new leaves when we are doing our 'normal' spring time potting.

Their main dormancy is during the hottest months. True, exotics are resting at this time as well, but it is not as deep as their winter sleep.

Another factor influencing their deep summer dormancy which usually occurs in December and January is that it is also the driest time, sometimes even to the extent of drought. At this time all the leaves are removed, the soil washed away and the roots severely pruned. If you find that your tree seems to be constantly growing you may have to artificially induce dormancy. This is done by allowing the soil to become dry to the point when the leaves start to wilt, thus simulating drought. The plant is then rootpruned either by bare rooting or removing the outer section of the root ball only. After replanting, the soil is kept well watered until new shoots appear.

Potting Mix. We use our basic mix irrespective of variety.

Fertilizer. In addition to the osmocote or nutricote at potting time, several times a year, wet the soil and apply about one teaspoon per medium size pot of either sulphate of ammonia or Aquasol sprinkled on top of the soil and watered in. Eucalypts seem to respond to large amounts of nitrogen. As well, we use our organic 'paste' autumn, winter and spring. The substitute would be blood and bone and fish emulsion at 4–6 weeks interval. Always wet the soil prior to fertilizing. Apply B&B at the rate of one teaspoon per medium size pot.

Styles. Excepting very Formal Upright (maybe it's possible) all styles are attainable. We even have a cascade.

Pruning. It is said that for every leaf on an Eucalypt, there is a dormant bud waiting to burst forth. If this is true, it would account for

Fig. 31 *An attractive miniature can be made,
especially with nicholii.*

their ability to seemingly 'come back from the dead'. That they can withstand drought, fire and massive insect attack makes it good Bonsai material, although excessive pruning is better done prior to the main growing season. Be more careful when pruning the heavily barked varieties, as it is more difficult for the shoots to penetrate the bark. With those varieties it is also safer to prune back to foliage. Varieties with the lignotuber respond more easily when pruning to bare wood.

An attractive miniature can be made, especially with nicholii, by obtaining a well advanced plant with a prominent lignotuber. Either in mid summer or prior to regrowth at some other time, cut away ALL the roots and trunk and branches growing out of the tuber, leaving only the potato like section. Choose a pot not much larger than the tuber, making sure that you remember where the soil level came to. It's possible to lightly press it into the soil, tying string around the pot and over the top of the tuber for stabilization until the roots become strong enough to support it. An abundance of branchlets will grow from the tuber, thin them out and keep the remainder trimmed to a triangular shape. As stated in the chapter on wiring, any upward growth from branches must be regarded as dangerous, and pruned either severely back, or cut right out. This cannot be emphasized enough. Eucalypts, more than any other species, is affected by this type of growth, and unless constant pruning is practised, attempts to alter the shape of the branches becomes almost impossible.

Trimming is a constant necessity as most varieties grow extremely fast. There is a tendency towards long internodal growth, so pinching out the new tips while they are still at an immature stage will help to reduce the length.

Wiring should not be a problem if the correct pruning techniques are followed.

Watering. Apart from extra water after repotting, we water the Eucalypts no differently to the other Bonsai.

Location. Sun or shade; can take light frost; most varieties can be exposed to coastal conditions.

FICUS
The Figs

Attraction. Massive trunks with buttressed bases and interesting aerial roots.

Suitability for Bonsai is unsurpassed. The very best tree for the beginner to practise with. Don't be discouraged by the size of the leaves, for with pruning and defoliation the most minute foliage can be obtained.

Varieties. Within Australia, there are abundant varieties suitable for Bonsai. It doesn't matter if you are unable to have it identified; the main criteria are smallish leaves which indicate short internodes and a trunk having the ability to enlarge at the base. The better known variety fitting that description is F. rubiginosa, the Port Jackson Fig, but the MOST FAMILIAR name known to most is F. Macrophylla, the Moreton Bay Fig. Irrespective of variety, the common practice is to call all Figs — Moreton Bays, which would be better discontinued.

Unfortunately, this Fig is not as suitable for several reasons. The natural size of the leaf is very large and pruning DOES cause a reduction, but its size indicates a worse defect difficult to correct i.e. LONG, COARSE INTERNODES. A further problem develops after trimming i.e. some branches have a tendency to die back. F. eugenoides, the Qld. Small leaf Fig is wonderful, but don't confuse it with F. hillii, another Qld. small leaf fig that is often trained into standards in tubs. The leaves are small but the trunk always remains thin. F. platypoda, named by Allan Cunningham, and given the common name of the Small-leaved Moreton Bay Fig, has the best feature of its big brother i.e. wide trunk base, but has smaller fruit and leaves, with shorter internodes. The Sandpaper Fig, F. coronata or F. stephanocarpa, as the common name implies, has an unusual rough surface on the leaves. The variety grows in damp areas which is indicated by its slender trunk. As the variety is worth working with, the thickening of the trunk will have to be acquired by growing and pruning techniques as described under Eucalypts — choice of material. Little white spots called hydathodes appear around the edges of most Fig leaves, although on some varieties they are more prominent than others. Their purpose is to secrete excess water. Very often people mistake them for scale.

Choice of material. Collecting is the most popular method for the enthusiast requiring a tree in a hurry. They can be found in trees such as palms, where bird droppings have deposited the seed. Look for them growing out of brick or stone walls and thriving in roof gutters. It may be difficult to obtain many roots from such areas, but with figs it doesn't seem to matter as long as the NIGHT temps. are at least 18–20°C. Plant into a box of sand until their roots have developed, then repot into your normal mix. Large trees are worth obtaining with trunk diameter in excess of 20 cm for they respond very well to carving.

To obtain a perfect miniature of our giant 'Moreton Bay Figs', the plant should be started from seed. This should be selected from a tree with a wide buttressed base, fine branches, short internodes and small leaves. Such a tree usually has small fruit. This should be collected when ripe, often picking up from the ground. As soon as possible, it should be squashed gently in a container of water to release the tiny seed. Care should be taken as each seed has a small hook, which, if removed, will fail to germinate. Allow everything to soak for a few days until fermentation begins. Everything floating is scooped away, and the seed on the bottom is drained and spread out to dry on newspaper. It is best stored in paper bags until required.

Sowing should not commence until the night temps. reach at least 20°C and can continue until Autumn. However, the earlier they are planted the more established they will be before the arrival of winter. The seed is sprinkled on TOP of the soil and only LIGHTLY covered with peat or sieved sphagnum. Figs can only germinate in light. The seedlings have to be protected from slugs and snails.

Figs exhibiting bulbous boles indicate that they have the capacity to withstand long periods of drought whether it be by climatic conditions, or location of germination i.e. up a palm tree or between rocks.

Fig. 32 *If you have a choice, select those that are wider at the base.*

53

Fig. 33 *Rounded boles can be improved by inducing roots to develop around the widest section.*

Seedlings with boles truly round and bulbous are not the most suitable to be used for Bonsai. If you have a choice, select those that are wider at soil level, becoming narrower up the 'trunk'. Rounded boles can be improved by inducing roots to develop around the widest section. This is done by inserting a narrow sharp knife slightly upwards into the cambium, and placing a fine stick or small pebble under the flap to keep it open. Either bury the incisions under the soil, or cover with sphagnum until the roots have grown.

Figs strike very easily from cuttings. Any excess branches removed from a Bonsai are worth trying. The top section of shortened stock even as large as 10 cm is suitable. A greater rate of success can be expected from cuttings taken from cultivated stock. Cuttings taken from the 'wild' may show a greater loss.

Trunks that have been developed from cuttings, tend to have less expansion at the base, although with time this can be overcome with good growing and pruning techniques.

As stated, figs that exhibit an expansive base are those that occur in naturally dry areas, or those that can tolerate long periods of drought. Their apparent capacity to store moisture for long periods could account for the stories one hears from time to time, about figs that have survived for months without attention. Aerial roots on some varieties disguise the fact that the main trunk is less buttressed, as the 'trunk' is composed of roots that become trunks after reaching the ground.

Grafting the smaller leaved varieties onto thick trunks of Moreton Bays is possible in summer. Aerial layering will also be successful.

Transplants with such ease during the warm months, that it is possible to change soil or pot many times during summer without setback.

Rootpruning. Can be bare rooted and severely cut back. Aerial roots, if unsightly, can be removed without loss of vigour to the tree. On the other hand, to encourage aerial roots, a humid atmosphere is needed, or the trunk and branches can be sprayed with water several times a day. Aerial roots develop during long periods of damp weather, and as the air becomes drier the tips dry out, and the root remains dormant until the next rainy spell. Placing your potted Fig on a brick or similar stand over a tray of water helps to create a humid environment. Attaching the dormant root onto a gauze bandage and placing the other end into the water, acts as a wick and the constant moisture induces the root to grow at an increased rate.

Potting Mix. Sand, soil and cow manure modified according to the varieties natural habitat. The naturally massive trunked Port Jacksons and Moreton Bays and to a lesser degree, the eugenoides benefit from extra drainage so more sand can be added. Slender trunked trees like hillii appreciate more humus. We have grown Figs in both acid and alkaline soil with no apparent difference.

Fertilizer. They are all massive feeders. Larger than normal amount of osmocote or nutricote is given at potting time. Our organic 'paste' is given monthly all year, as for the past few years, the figs have continued to grow through the winter in most areas of Sydney.

Styles. Figs are suitable for all styles, even cascades with no loss of vigour. They are particularly suited for rock plantings.

Pruning. Severe reduction, cutting back to bare wood and extensive carving can be successfully carried out during the warmer months. To help thicken branches, the growing tip is allowed to extend without trimming until the required thickness is obtained. Any vertical shoots growing at the base near the trunk, or along the branch need not be removed, as this will not affect and weaken any horizontal growth.

Contrary to most trees, Figs tolerate being top pruned and rootpruned drastically when there is new growth on the tree.

Trimming. The aim of all Fig growers is to obtain a crown of small leaves, in fact it could almost become a cult. This aim is easily achieved by correct trimming. Defoliation of course is one way, but if the leaves are removed too early in the season, the next crop may be as large as the original. We start to cut off the leaves in mid summer around the week after Christmas, and sometimes continue well into autumn (April). Districts experiencing frost may be advised to cease in early autumn (March).

Small leaves can be acquired without leaf pruning simply by cutting back the new shoots, leaving only the first leaf on each elongation. It works this way. After a shoot has been trimmed, the first leaf is rather small, and each leaf following, becomes successively larger, so, by removing all except the first, the pattern of the foliage is cut-a leaf, cut-a leaf and so on until the only leaves on the tree are small ones in between trimmed stalks.

Fig.34 *The first leaf is rather small
and each leaf following becomes
successively larger, so, by
removing all except the first.*

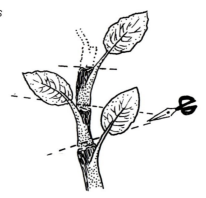

Fig. 35 *Cut-a leaf, cut-a leaf —*

The milky sap that oozes from cuts will cease if the cuts are sprayed with water.

Wiring is easy and the wood very pliable, taking extreme bending. By flexing a branch a few times to the position you wish it to take can often be achieved without wiring.

Location. Figs are one of the few species that can be kept indoors for longer periods, but do not return them outdoors to hot summer sun immediately, otherwise burning may occur.

Some Figs can tolerate slight frosts without harming the leaves. If heavy frosts occur in your district, the Figs must be given shelter during the winter.

Figs thrive along the coast under salty conditions.